This collection has a dose of meditative p
on the colonial and neoliberal foundation
from nature and allow rapacious extracti
criminalization of environmental defende
with survival struggles with no life boughs. **These are poems that call for action.**

This volume of poems affirms Nnimmo Bassey's stature as one of Africa's ardent campaigners for environmental justice and ultimate triumph over global oil mafias and profiteers. The poems pulsate with compassion and audacious optimism about human resilience and the future. The images, stories and reflections are animated by stubborn hope and prophetic vision that predict the end of the world's oil and gas empires. The poet summons a global coalition to arise and redeem our Earth and its plundered plenitude. As the poet assures us, "after oil, we flourish" because "we are seeds planted, we sprout, blossom and bud..."

— G. G. Darah
Professor of Oral Literature, Folklore and Cultural Sciences

Nnimmo Bassey's life is poetry. It is like lyrics of the earth because he is one with the earth — straddling at once many different spaces and living in perfect symbiosis with and within the spaces that his ancestors bequeathed to him.

In *I See The Invisible* his wordsmanship comes through as a rich offering overflowing with earth wisdom, ancestral wisdom and the flowery narrative that Africans have developed over millennia. He echoes the songs from the daily struggles of honest folk, in the determined farming of smallscale farmers and in the pathos of disappointed communities.

— Ibrahima Thiam
author of "Doxandem"

Nnimmo Bassey is a deep person who drives action and allows others to question themselves.

— Houmi Ahamed-Mikidache
Journalist, ERA ENVIRONNEMENT

Many injustices remain invisible to us, but Nnimmo Bassey is the rare witness who not only sees them, but compels us to do so through the power of his imagination and empathy. Nnimmo's unsparing gaze as a witness spares none of the injustices affecting our world: whether it is environmental devastation in the Niger Delta, the unfair allocation of resources due to corruption, or the violence that draws from base instincts. Contemplative and reflective, *I See The Invisible* forces the reader to take off the blinkers and stare at our collective future, with his words offering us hope.

— Salil Tripathi
Writer – Journalist – Human Rights Busybody, Books: *Offence: The Hindu Case* (Seagull 2009), *The Colonel Who Would Not Repent* (Aleph 2014, Yale 2016), *Detours: Songs of the Open Road* (Tranquebar 2015).

Reading the new book with poetry by Nnimmo Bassey is a breathtaking experience. Making you see the invisible is the magic Nnimmo exercises on the reader. It left me with the perception of another world. A world of despair, hope, integrity and unconditional love.

— Hans van Willenswaard
Right Livelihood College, Bangkok

I see the Invisible
see the Invisible
the Invisible
Invisible

nnimmo
bassey

Daraja Press

Published by
Daraja Press
https://darajapress.com

Cover design by Otoabasi Bassey, BASE-X

Library and Archives Canada Cataloguing in Publication
Title: I see the invisible / Nnimmo Bassey.
Names: Bassey, Nnimmo, author.
Identifiers: Canadiana 20230572618 | ISBN 9781990263897 (softcover)
Subjects: LCGFT: Poetry.
Classification: LCC PR9387.9.B37 I2 2023 | DDC 821/.92—dc23
Printed and bound by CPI Group (UK) Ltd, Croydon, CR0 4YY

Dedication

To all chroniclers of hope

Author's Note

Truth be told, I never thought I would write another volume of poetry after the last, **I will not Dance to Your Beat** (2011). The reason was that my previous volumes were reactive to circumstances of the times. **Patriots and Cockroaches** (1992) was a reaction to the socio-political corruption that had engulfed Africa and dimmed the enthusiasm that had been built by the years of struggle for independence. Whereas we thought we were stepping into a post colonial era, what we stepped into was vicious neo colonial times. The next collection, **Poems on the Run** (1995) was a reaction to military autocracy and the repression that followed. The volume was literally written underground. This was followed by **Intercepted** (1998) all written while detained at *Kalakuta Republic* of Alagbon Close. **We Thought it was Oil But it was Blood** (2002) responded to two things primarily - extractivism and the accompanying human and environmental rights abuses in the Niger Delta and elsewhere. The massive erosion of biodiversity and attacks on food sovereignty through the introduction of genetically modified organisms (GMOs) into our agricultural system inspired **I Will not Dance to your Beat**.

What you have in your hands, or on your screens, is a compilation that is largely more meditative than the previous collections. There are moments of reflection on the colonial and neoliberal foundations that permit a willful disconnection from nature and the resultant destructive extractivism.

Some of the poems came through conversations and poetry writing sessions with Peter Molnar, Maryam al-Khawaja – Rafto Human Rights laureates and Salil Tripathi, a member of the board of PEN International, in August 2017. The sessions held at a beautifully rustic location in Celleno, Italy, were documented on celluloid by the duo of Maria Galliana Dyrvik and Anita Jonsterhaug Vedå of SMAU, a multimedia firm in Norway. Poetic relationship with Maria and Anita has continued over the years and their work continues to inspire more and more poems.

We have also had time to ponder on the criminalization of environmental defenders and burdening of victims with survival struggles with no life boughs. The poems were written over a wide span of time and require some pondering as poems often demand, of course. Although written over a broad time spectrum, they fall into identifiable themes. The harsh times that birthed the earlier volumes were blunted with doses of humour as poetry is largely therapeutic and contributes to our wellness and wellbeing.

In our communities poetry and song are key tools for exposure of ills in our societies, for education and for rebuke. Poetry is an indispensable cultural tool with which we laugh at the wicked and add the needed bounce to our steps as we march on to end ecocide and give our people and other beings a chance to retain our being. The call of this volume is that we must ensure that *we see the invisible and hear the inaudible.*

Nnimmo Bassey

Contents

Our Soul

Mother Earth our Teacher

Schooled by Nature
I understood the pains of motherhood.
Painful sights under flailing limbs
Logs in batteries floating upstream
The swinging axe of fellows addicted to capital
Spares not the iroko or the mahogany or the unwary squirrels.
Schooled by experience
I comprehend complexities through rationality.
The things that hide behind the things that
Make the unthinkable suddenly desirable
Like burning Papa's house to inherit the ashes.
Unfathomable beauty rages
Counter to infernal acts of inhumanity.
Pumping crude into the common creek
And hoping to distil pure water by barricading oxygen from the
    nostrils of the dispossessed
To wed hydrogen to power new dimensions of greed.
Yet we labour to reproduce our given hope
In the crucible of repressed desires.
Teachings by Mother Earth the educator
Liberates on the canvass of fresh sensibilities
We couldn't be so impervious
That we forget who holds us up
That we forget who fires us up
That we forget who empowers us
To comprehend our humanity.
Not cowed humanity without spine
We crave a humanity dressed in dignity and respect
Cross cultural chasms and on the
highway of learning and social progress

Scarified and sacrificed

You walked over my head
Through the open door of my heart
My welcome was my death
Scarified and sacrificed
Here lies the remains of my home
Militarised and brutalised
There lie the bleached bones of my territory
Conflict minerals
Doused in blood of two legged men and many legged relatives.
Here lie the remains of critical minerals at a critical moment
Disempowered by the impetus to batter for batteries on distant shores
Now here is the lie
The criminal minerals exhumed from the labyrinth
Polished and purified seven times of the dregs that were its life
Waved over strange fires and lodged on wagging tongues
Here is the truth in the lie
The sparkling bars cast a million shadows
But are dead

The Womb of the Earth

Thousands of serpentine tubes
Suck dry the womb of the Earth
Leaving hollow echo chambers
Of pain, tears and blood.
We stagger as tremors rock the land
And rifts widen between
Man and corporate beasts.
Capital denies even slivers of thought
That Mother Earth abhors vacuums.
Strapped on the slab
Gasping for poisoned air
Bled to death
You announce a divorce
You claim to divest
To deny your guilt
You pull a worn magician's cloak
Yet we will never forget
The bowels you've slit
The children you've drowned
The grandmothers you have stolen.
You lie.
The children are awake
We hear their songs
In sync with bouncing steps
They won't be stopped
They will not stop
Until you pay the debt

Choked by Convenience

Convenience and Greed
The two thieves between whom
We are nailed
Shall we forgive them
Seeing they know exactly what they are doing?
Held high as cheap
Hoisted aloft as efficient
We got enamoured
Denuded
Spat upon
Slapped
Our dignity dragged in oceans of crude
Our pride roasted on the fiery furnaces of oily companies

Convenience and Greed
The two thieves between whom
We are sacrificed
We drown in mountains of plastic
As plastics swallow the world
Whales, crocs, hippos and the tiny ones
Feast on the sheets of their last suppers
Cattle, sheep, rabbits, goats, antelopes and hapless kids
Lie prostrate fed on fatal plastic lies
Postmortems denied
Funerals delayed
Paid mourners weeping tearless howls

Convenience and Greed
The two thieves between whom
We are wrapped
Here lies the deaf generation
Wedded to the catwalks of lies
Who denied the shouts from Mother Earth
Addicted to efficient destruction

Bedevilled by ease
Addicted to speed
A world on a mad dash to the tipping point
Roaring temperatures
Ragging floods
Roaring fires
Maddening droughts
Desertified deserted lands
Oceanified polluted swamps
Eyes open, arms linked
We build the barricades
Solidarity erases greed
A time to embrace the inconvenient
And heed the call of Mother Earth

I'm Not Afraid

I dread the creeks
I dread the swamps
The streams
The lagoons
The ocean
Coated by your crude filth

I hold my breath
I live with infernal thirst
The wind
The fruits
The tubers
Loaded with your toxic murk

I see your heinous claws
I see your bloodied fangs
I see your putrid harvests
I am coming for you
I am not afraid
Of you

I come from the future

Pardon me if I'm impatient with history
I come from the future
Rooted in the soil
I recall the toil
And never recoil
From the struggles to defend Nature
Fixated on the innermost core
That built your past
And sincerely is what will last
Pardon me if I'm impatient with history
My turf is to awake memories
Tenderly built by generosity
I recall the utter perplexity
Of those who revel in complexity
Building logs of life sapping stories
Woven by beings totally at variance with Nature
But I come from the future
Borne by memories of love and fires
Powered by a knowing that drives desires
And strengthened by those unseen wires
That codify and connect our culture
Fixated on the sacred seed
To build the dream future we need

Recent Ancients Foretold

The waves crash, roll and roar
At the shore lines of distant dreams
The waters tease beaches hopes
You should be beneath me they hum
Those rolls and tamping roils
And the suspect caressing of the sands
The whispering of lulling tunes yet unsung
A dream once retold
Above the expanse of the airy sea above our heads
We swim in the air aiming for the stars
As they twinkle and sparkle directed by Mission Control freaks
Objects seen in the firmament
Are larger than they seem
Larger than the specks fitting the Earth
Yet some are smaller than they boast they are
Like
Blots fighting futile battles over territories
Annihilating, displacing, dispossessing the weak the starving
and the sick
As the ancients foretold
The sea rises altering the maps
Knocking on sleepy bald heads
While the mass get shoved to the tipping point rise
Chocked on carbonated airs
Yet we hear rebellious songs
Songs and throngs rising, songs of
Warming long foretold
Paddling the air over warming seas
What you hear is larger than what you see
Do you see the laughing waves
Bouncing and trumping the shores
Do you hear the wounded crab hiding in the sand
The maddened mudskippers bereft of mud
And the dazed frogs that skipped the proverbial pan

While men jump from pan into yawning ovens
It is the dawn
The recent ancients foretold

Horizon

The horizon never leaves
Yet even at full throttle
Even on full solar tanks
None could reach her

The horizon never leaves
Yet she is so aloof
Even when the sky kisses the sea
None could grasp her

The horizon is never rough
Her perfect curve
The arc of her back
None could find a toehold

The horizon is never uncertain
Constant as the northern star
She dances on the edges of our eyes
None could ignore her

The horizon is loudly clear
Even on misty days she is there
Wedged on our imagination
She is the eternal lighthouse

The Other Side

Always wondered what it would mean
To see the other side of the moon
The face on the persistent side isn't mean
Still I wonder if she smiles would I swoon?
Get this moon to rotate or toss me another
The fireball of a sun doesn't smoother
Though we peek at the flaming ball of fire
As we twirl and twist not as a matter of desire
But because the equation has long been concluded
And don't think I somehow colluded
With our Maker who made the moon and hid the side
That now torments my quivering mind as I slide
Less than a speck in the constellation
Stars, meteors and junk satellites watch in consternation
And huge invisible to the biggest eyes
Cannot see the imaginary ice
Mummified on imaginary longitudes of the lunar
Despite light years of uncanny slumber.
The question about which side of the sun
Is the hottest
Is not a matter for idle chatter, contest or protest
But that about the hidden abodes of lunatics
I beseech thee not even satellites of plastics
Will let the matter rest in peace or on the sea
And wave on the unwavering odyssey

I like those bridges

I like those bridges
With see-through guard rails
But I don't really mind the monstrous
Concrete barricades
That keep my eye from seeing
The Niger
The Nun
The Orashi
The Qua Iboe
The Focardos.
Truth is
I would prefer transparent rails and
Transparent bridges
So I could see the fisher
Pulling away in the dugouts or
Throwing the net in those
Extravagant flairs of hope
That today yield nothing
Except for the ubiquitous plastics
Flying from exotic cars.
Even truer
I am happy for opaque bridges
And impenetrable eye rails
For last time I craned my selfie stick
Of a neck to peer
At the creek
I was weak
And shed a tumbler full of tears
As dead fish
And sundry relatives
Floated on a bed of crude
And an assortment of putrid aromas
Threw me off my seat
Or was it my feet

Barricades

I come at your barricades
Or you emerge from the heap of trash
Guns raised
Finger on the trigger
Palms open begging
Yielding exact change
For the bribe extracted

I came to our barricades
At every blind corner
Or you emerge from every pothole
Nay, crater
Captive trapped in the cracks
I watch as you squint at my papers
Wondering how you
Manage to read with the sheets
Upside down
And your head between your legs

I see you at every market
Pure water.
Kpekere
Kpokpo garri
Skewered maggots
Monkey nuts
Bananas
I could sit on your pile of rubbish
And have a state dinner
Watching
The extortionist in you
Squeeze hapless road farers

I see your multiple
Placemarkers

On the highway of distress
I see you yet I come from point to point
Answering tepid questions
Wishing you had hot numbers
Shocked you speak only one language
At the cue of coins

I see you at every crossing
Of pipelines laid by the polluters
From the belly of belching dragons
Were you paid to watch the rotten pipes
Were you hired to guard the heinous furnaces
Or you paid to steal my peace
Block my way
Wink at oil thieves
Perched on your pile of trash
Checking your balances
Behind tattered sandbags?

I come at your barricades
Or you emerge from the heap of trash
Flesh of the poor trapped between
Your teeth
You feast on sorrows
You swim neck deep in pools of tears
You merciless hooligans
Who dare to tag my children
Restive
And if you were resting
How come you parade missing buttons
Laceless boats
And are laced with guns and batons?

I see you at every crossing
Of pipelines laid by the polluters
But your eyes are on

My pockets
You toothless mouth mouthing
Profanities
As though the chant
Invokes your payday
You think you are killing me
You
A zombie
Rejected by the dead

Rising Smoke

We saw the rising smoke
A signal rising in the sky
A banner of victory
For pipe bursters
Or it may be
That this one
Played cricket
On a soccer pitch
The accomplices scored a hit
And notched one more number
Of errant bush laboratories
Playing the hard ball
The game went past extra time
And now in the sudden death
Poor villagers gasp
Choke
Fall
Like flies

Secured

Security men
With rocket launchers
Stop you
And
You won't stop?
Security men
With the pin off
Grenades
Stop you
And
You won't stop?
Security men
In combat fatigue
And tear gas canisters
Just shot one for withholding a few coins
Stop you
And
You won't stop?

Static Drip

If 1956 was a year on your calendar
1958 was an exclamation mark.
On one your stabs spurted
On the other your loot sailed the ocean
To oil your fat vats
And grease your deep pouches.
1937, the entire land was your playground.
Dusters, dry wells and toxic piles
We're mere shells broken in search of the proverbial omelette.
Your rigs rigged our lives
Floating platforms mocked us in tales long foretold
The water we took to quench our thirst
Quenched and entombed us in your colourful sludge
Your insatiate serpentine entrails
Stripped our lands
Fouled our waters
Messed up the air
All the while
Dealing hopes
On static drip

Aloof

Aloof
We disconnect from each other
And retreat into our cocoons

Aloof
We dodge slogans hurled at each other
Like mortars fired from cracked canons

Aloof
We speak past our ears and over our heads
Ridiculing, demonising and shaming each other

Aloof
We build castles and amass weapons of self suffocation
Shivering in the heat, derelict in our aloneness

We are the moon and the sun

We are the moon and the sun
We rise above rising temperatures
We swim against rising tides

We are the wind and the clouds
We are not bound by statistics
We know you may name but not hold the clouds

We are the flowers and the seeds
We fertilize the soils and flood our tables
We deodorize the sweat that attend our labours

We are the voice and the memory
We reject enticements to forget our manacles
We resist and overturn forces of oppression

We are the delta and we are the swamp
We welcome and we habour multiple species
We are those whose homes are now in the sea

We are the migrants and we ride the waves
We are the itinerant stomping flaming Sahara
We will convert of your rigs into wind farms

We are the sounds and we are the sights
We wake you up and we lull you to sleep
We tell you to hear the ringing bells of liberation

I

Our Inspiration

Love

Love is
The big question no one answers
Except you
Is love
Lost in the clouds
Raised by dancing feet
And fleeting smiles
And hidden chuckles
When you are alone.
You never fail to wriggle
Out of the fool's clutches
And how would you
Seeing the fool believes
That love
Is blind

Gratitude

Standing under your lofty canopy
I am humbled by your countless birthmarks
How many have sheltered under your foliage
So many you have housed the fluttering ones in their citadels
Sitting on your roots
I ponder the depth of your generosity
You don't bark at those who peck your bark
You feed
You heal
You speak wisdom to listening ears
You whistle timeless hymns as
The wind rustles through your hair
Standing under your lofty canopy
I ponder the mystery of your exhalations
That powers my inhalations

There is beauty

There is beauty
On every page
When it its blank .
A million universes before your eyes
Hold back the nib
Nib those thoughts at the bud
Offer me blank pages
There is beauty
On every page
When it its blank.
Before the inks
Drip
And the link
Is torn
And the poem
Is done

Twilight

There is a shaft of light
that slices through the leaves
Herald of the awaited dawn or
Town crier of a cruel dusk
Caught in the twilight
Sharing slices of the dark
Calling the arrival
Or departure
Of flocks
Of owls of bats of weavers
Of sunbirds
And of predators
Called men
Caught in bloated greed

Hill Huggers

Serpentine hill huggers
A dream of tree huggers
But let me crawl to shades guarded by shafts of light
Amidst the gurgling brook

Ensconced in the steep lipped saucer
I peer up and scarcely see where your crown lays
Dwarfed men beneath towering
We step gingerly, silently
Into the cathedral grove

Knock knock knock
Who would be in
Your hollowed out belly
Surely not the woodpecker
Your cavern a door into millennia long gone

Swamp Buggies

Swamp buggies
Share
Cracked up roads with hawkers
Of hamburgers
As we jostle on expressways
Crazily sent into space
As rocket from the launchpads of
Potholes yet to be tracked by google map

If you like those bridges
Get a hovercraft
To safely sail
On the highway
Above Martian caters
Above ubiquitous secured
Choke points

Bumping into the Wind

Maybe your hand is too short to touch the air
Even on tiptoe you cannot see beyond your hair
But can you even see the wind
Though you hear it howl and see the spin
It must be exasperating when the air blows through your hair
Parting the strands and exposing you have but just a pair.

I chuckle as you keep bumping into the air
Erasing from your scalp what some could count as hair

Maybe the fishes do see
water as they swirl in the sea
Or why would the dolphin jump into the air
Do they seek to deny humans their share
Of the air with chief accomplice in the flying fish
That blithely avoids the chef's petri dish

But if the tilapia hidden in caverns in the sea only feels
The water as it glides over its gills.

What if the community of fishes do not see the water
Should I then worry if the air before my eyes does not waver
As we inch closer to leaving the murky puddle
Does that get us any less entangled in the riddle
That keeps you bumping into the wind
And the tilapia seeing your hook sighs how unkind

Thinking you are a fish you jump into the sea
Fishes agree all creatures are one, but seeing a predator they flee
And I watch perched on transparent ice cube
As you jump into a fiercely scattered group
A scattered group stuck in rarified air
In a place for which you have no flair

Mangled Mangroves

Sit here for a while
As I ponder the sea
Wondering if the sardines
Were sad being refused a place
In the mangled roots
Of absent mangroves
And astonished earthworms couldn't
Warm to the thoughts
Of concretized wetlands

Rainbows on the Sea

Rainbows are beautiful when in the sky
Colourful promise of peace
Announcing the end of floods

Knee deep in the crude
Why Probe the skies
When flood awaits on tidal waves of the dead creeks

Look down alarmed
Death by stealth is vivid in the many colours
Of floating crude

The blinding sheen of the rainbow curves
Racing on the back of plastics and stubborn bones
Seeking unwary throats that dare the deadly broth

Stilts and Wiggles

Sometimes perplexed
By how your resolve to love and not to be vexed
For though you love the waves of the sea
It seems you see farther than anyone else could see
You fight for lands that men annex
Not a care about your duty of care so clear if complex
Yet you continue to hold the soil
And refuse to move into the sea or recoil
To allow the sea a passage to the land
Though you obviously know their plan
All to protect profligate men determined to simply spoil
Your roots for fire and for timber which they stick into the soil
While wielding axes with handles made from your stem
In the faulty metrics of a cannibal system
Deaf to your cries of pain
They continue to bite your roots for their gain
Yet you stand stately on stilts a sight for weary eyes
A joy for the wiggly and feathery ones certain you hear their cries
Sometimes perplexed
By mindless so-called territories reclamations and annexed
The nurseries the stately ones provide
By how the wiggly ones dance in the sea but keep to the divide
Hopping atimes above the waves to see the shore
Beating the fellows who swore
That you would hop into the bobbing boat
Or take the skewered worms seeking your throat
You aren't attracted by the fires on the shore
I see you dance between the thighs the stuff of lore
Who love to see the sea and often longingly peep
But take a strategic stand away from the deep
I'm one with you both, the wiggly and the stately one
Assured that we have our limits but thankfully share one sun

The Stump I So Loved

The stump I so loved
Was a reminder of a tree
I could only see through others that stood
With roots intertwined and
wondering where went the branches,
Where went the leaves and the fruits.

The stump I so loved
Held the ground on the brow
Or would you say on the lips
Of the creek
The creek swole and ebbed
Yielding futile hopes of mudskippers
Barracuda, snappers and catfish
If what I hear is true.
But my people don't lie as they know
The crocodiles, the periwinkles and oysters
Were part of their stories, songs and life
And indeed almost members of the clan.

The stump I so loved
Was my sacred spot connecting
My vision of marred Mother Earth
And my sacred resolve to be one with her.
This was my sacred spot
Deep breaths, wheezy gulps
Teary eyes, running nose
Thanks to the toxic loads
From the infernal lords.

The stump I so loved
Held the running soil
And got stumped by my incessant perch
Enshrouded sometimes by shorts, shirts and wrappers as

Kids trusted and gleefully took a dive
Under the sheen and emerged with
Glittering skins and soon lost weight
From the load of heavy metals
Gulped as they wiggled and somersaulted in
The dreary toxic soup.

The stump I so loved
Is gone
Too soon
Like the giggles of the boys and girls
Whose lives have been well and utterly spent
Erased and interred with no farewell songs
By the lords of everything crude-
Whether oil
Gas or coke.

The stump I so loved
Has left
It's memory sparks not even a ripple
No, not a wiggle
As I stand gazing
At desolate yonder bank
Lined with stumps
Of ghostly trees

Contemplation

How beautiful a transition can be
If it is the point of no return
How inspiring could sleep be
If it is not a point of invisible activity
(if it is not a point of disappearance)
How inspiring could an inhalation be
If it is more than a transition to exhalation
How beautiful can death be
If it means rising never to die again

Beads of Inspiration

Seeds of inspiration
Spread faster than pollen grains
Like sand caught between the toes

Beads of perspiration
Float faster than mud slides
Like water caught on a duck's back

If you don't agree
Go to court!

Astonished monkeys

Astonished monkeys mope
At passing cars
Wondering will they stop
To drop a banana now
They have destroyed the forests

Long legs yield patronage
Maybe connections
But long necks beckon
The slaughter
Ask the giraffe

Imaginations don't run wild
In the wild
Youngsters on forlorn search
As they shepherd the flock
In wastelands
Once full of life

Colourful, colourful yes
The parrots, the sunbird, the weavers
And even the crow
Flutter and dive into
Oily lakes
Now you've made your kill

Seducing the Bees

I watched your back as you danced
The ripples of the beats pulsating in your swings
Your dance always magic
Your dance so intimate
I watched your elegant steps as the drums called
I watched as you danced between the iroko
Your dance mesmerised the butterflies
Your dance seduced the bees
Then I realised I was dancing
With the entire room
Then I realised I was dancing
In the Milky Way
On a speck amidst the galaxies

Our Sight

What We Behold

(For Orin Langelle)

The joy of a peek through the keyhole
Is built on the imaginaries your eyes behold
The click and the flash
Yield awesome knowing where minds clash
Seeing with one eye shut
That's the amazing gem that erupts before the cut
I wonder how you see what others ignore
The overburdened lad whose dream is a quiet spot for a snore
The hapless worker who labours all day and night
Yet none applauds the inexhaustible store of her might
And what about the madness that makes humans see everything
As game for manipulation without thinking
Deluded to think they can make Mother Earth more efficient
Men tinker with seeds the core of life, claiming they are beneficent
And now they aim for the sky, the seas, the lands ignoring they are
    not omniscient
Absent minded pursuit of capital blinds any thoughts of the present

The joy of a peek through the keyhole
Is built on the imaginaries your eyes behold
The click and the flash
Yield awesome knowing where minds clash
Seeing with one eye shut
Life played out real and uncut
The things we don't see
The things we wont see
Places on the blocks of thought
Nothing sold or bought
Pushing through the hard soils of calloused hearts
Deftly avoiding the fiery darts
Of impudent men
Harbingers of that deadly omen
To which we never holler Amen!

Still I wonder how you see what others ignore
Is it that we had walked this way before
Or we are complicit in the deadly rat race
That has long left many in that mindless endless chase?

The joy of a peek through the keyhole
Is long lasting if you are not sucked into the peephole
Or even the manhole
And if you remain whole
Knowing that being is nothing if you are all alone
Ignoring the billions of relatives on land, sea and sky
Never deaf to the groaning of the oppress and even their howling cry
A shot in the dark
A nap in the park
A coin in the pocket
Your eyeball still in its socket
Snap
Clap
They may not present a plaque
Know they are sure glad you've got their back.
Snap
Clap
Strap
Map
The joys of many peeks through the keyhole
The deep knowing that victory comes from what we do with
what we behold.

Power!

Driven to the cliff edge
The world clings to power from fossilized forests
Sitting on a dangerous ledge
Fossil mafias hold out when necessary on turrets
Resisting power from wind, water and the sun
They posit that power from these cannot crank heavy machineries
Reality shrouded in mysteries and powered by crafted scorn
They insist best power comes from capacity to multiply miseries
Pray is one kilowatt of power from coal different from same measure
From wind or what indeed powers this deadly insistence though
    the planet gets hotter?
It seems dear people it is all about power to keep the pressure
Ensuring private control is impossible with the sun, wind or water.
Believe it or not, some individuals and corporations do not
    give a hoot
As long as people and territories can be sacrificed
And care naught if the planet burns provided they can increase the
    piles of their loot
In the coal mines fists got raised to halt deadly exploitation of labour
    often contrived
With oil and gas serpentine pipes and armadas of ocean going vessels
Trash ecosystems, choke the air amid false claims they can sequester
Carbon furiously burned and spewed as though driven by devils
Today the alarm bells ring from every quarter
Asking if one kilowatt power from oil is different from same measure
From the sun or what indeed powers this willful suffocation?
Indeed the struggle for just energy transition calls for all necessary
    pressure
For this is a battle for energy democracy and popular liberation.

I see the invisible

I see the invisible
I hear the inaudible
I feel the intangible

I'm everywhere in no time
Floating on memories of strained futures
Aloft on lofty hopes
Sliding on rugged dreams in truncated nights

I see the invisible
I hear the inaudible
I feel the intangible

Ears on the ground we tremble
At the departing footsteps of
Departed elders at marketplaces

I see the invisible
I hear the inaudible
I feel the intangible

Eyes on the past we see the future
Cluttered by discarded viruses and their angry relatives
Hands glued to our sides social distances narrow to a kilometre apart

I see the invisible
I hear the inaudible
I feel the intangible

We have never been closer now we are apart
Finally, nature's tiny beings shake sleep away
We are relatives and can have a good day
If we don't scoff and cough in each other's face

Things Not Seen

Hebrews 11:1 (KJV, NLT, MSG)

Now
faith is the substance
of things hoped for,
the confidence that
what we hope for will happen
The assurance about
things we cannot see
the evidence of things not seen.
By it
the people in days of old
earned a good report
Got a good reputation.
This distinguished our ancestors,
It set them above the crowd.

Portals of Greed

The portals of greed
Pain, misery and death
Constantly open up for
More travellers on the highway to hell
Enmeshed in the euphoria
Of numbed flotations
All are sold for a pinch
A snort
A drag
A puff
A jab
That drags to the dead to the portal that
Blasts open exhilarating chasms
That sell a pleasure measured in minutes
Or when generous may lasts the breath of sleep
But dissipates with a blink of empty sockets
From which no eyes peep.

Looter's Boulevards

Street names sometimes stab at the heart
Men whose heads should be bowed by shame
Or whose heads should be adorned with dust
Were we to learn of the unconscionable deeds
Including the erasure from history of many they maimed

Names of autocrats
Named after murderers
And even petty thieves

And those that stole elections
And hang their photos on every tree
Bearing excellencies, honorables
And other epithets too unbearable
Like the wigs adorning empty heads

Names of autocrats
Named after murderers
And even petty thieves
No wonder
These are
One way boulevards
To getting lost

Cast a Vote

As I cast my vote I knew
It carried my dream
Now I sit to relish some last poems
By Olav H. Hauge the farmer & poet
And wait for the deluge
The flood of results
When some will dance
And others wince

What Would You See?

Have you ever wondered what you would see
If your eyes were to look inwards
Would it unveil your mind
Or would you mind what you see
And what if the eyes you roll keep rolling and wouldn't stop till they climb the log
Or what if they rolled out of the sockets and crossed the moat

Would you then see the folds of your brain
And decipher why your thoughts get trapped
In the milk of your scattered brain

But if your eyes rolled and rolled and rolled
Until they found their way into your brain
Would you then see the futility of all that pain
Endured as you battled to train
Your eyes to focus on the black dot
That blurs the link
Between your sight and your appetite
Between your eyes and your stomach
Between your tears and your dusty saliva

Would you then see the folds of your brain
And decipher why your thoughts get trapped
In the mire of your scuttled brain

Have you ever wondered what you would see
If your eyes were to look inwards
Would it unveil your mind
Or would you mind what you see
And what if the eyes you roll keep rolling and wouldn't stop
Or what if they rolled out of the sockets
And into your empty pockets

Would you then see the tales told of your brain
And decipher why your thoughts get scrapped
In the lobe of your shuttered brain

Political Will

If only we had buckets full of political will
By now we would be at El Dorado

A cover all statement
When we are not ready for settlement
There is a lack of Political will!
Folks shout when they so feel
Till they climb the giant wheel
Of leadership dancing on banana peels
Crazy bald heads with eyes in sunken sockets
Committed to sating their bottomless pockets

Grassroots battalion stump their feet and snort
Bring the brats let's string them for sport
The demands for change fills the air
But only few would a thought spare
In the babble none would for a moment pause
To join hands and truly fight for the cause
The demand for leadership hooked on the common good
Fizzles out once the top goon emerges from our neighbourhood

Justice denied
For lack of political will
Security unattained
For lack of political will
Corruption multiplies
For lack of political will
Leadership comatose
For lack of political will
Crime's skyrocket
For lack of political will
Colonialism prevails
For lack of political will

If only we had buckets full of political will
By now we would be at El Dorado

A cover all statement
When we are not ready for settlement
There is a lack of Political will!
Folks shout when they so feel
Till they climb the giant wheel
Of leadership dancing on banana peels
Crazy bald heads with eyes in sunken sockets
Committed to sating their bottomless pockets
Yet the battle cry ebbs in a whimper
Once the ear is tuned to the wicked whisper

If only we had ears tuned to the wailings of the sunken cheeks
By now we would be far off the wicked creeks

This Hate does not define us

Mangled ballot boxes
Bloodied faces
Headless goats
Mouthy hoodlums in the corridors of power
Burning votes define the
Last (s)elections

Yes the (s)election has come
Yet refuses to go

You are not us
We are not you
Stay away!
Risk death
If you won't thumb my avatar
Meanwhile the powerful masquerade as enemies
In the dark they snort together
Convivial cannibal crooks feasting on
Laden tables

Yes the (s)election has come but
When will it be gone

The loquacious wax louder
Brimming bile and utter nonsense
The Good Book declares
Even fools are thought wise when they keep silent;
with their mouths shut, they seem intelligent.
Maggots-laden mouths lie in wait
To spew more trash on the threshing floors of death

Hate does not define us

Still hate struts bloodied streets propelled
On ballistic missiles
Stereotypes misfired from damned guns
Cheap commodities for bloody blackmail

But
This hate does not define us

Yes the (s)election has come but
Yet refuses to go.
Yes, we voted, weeping, dancing, beaten by rain and batons
Yes, voters waited outside the nameless collation tombs.

Why are dancers frozen in midair?
And winners blowing muted trumpets?

Written after reading Bishop Kukah's Easter message

Our Fight

Duty Bound

It can be beautiful watching mounting
Anxieties of the undelivered bag
Hung thick over the conveyor belt.
Necks craned in rhythmic twists
Eyes peeled like of predators about to strike
Devotees watch as dreams of tokens
Fly by.
Echoes of sauntering steps
In the twisted cavernous multicoloured
Scented duty-free alleys
Quicken dreams
Sold by low priests of capital and
Retailers of greed entrap the unwary and
Insatiate and addicted accumulators of
Junk
Duty bound by vacuous promises of embraces.

By Me We Spoke

Stolen
Across swollen waters
To you, thousands of us were
Pieces of wood, tusks, brass
Merchandise
To tickle the fancies of heartless merchants and enablers of violence
But you were wrong.
A heist of brass and wood and ivory
Murderous desecration of our revered palaces
Over hundred years and you are yet to nod in sleep
Slowly your crimes seek you out.
Secured in mounted cells I wonder
What you learn when you grope my bloodless frame
In contrived musings in citadels of stealing
Knowing you cannot know me on the altars of twisted history?

Gawking
Dumbstruck
Awestruck at the loving work of ancestral masters
You derided them
Vilified cultures of justice
Burnt, smashed, raped and plundered all night
You drank my blood.
Setting off before cockcrow
You couldn't imagine that *akukor*
Will still crow years after entombment in your armoured cases.

Grabbed
Thousands of market days ago
I was denied regal splendour of ethical multiversities
In the ancient kingdoms where thieving was strictly outlawed
Who would dare the gods to be a thief?
Wrapped in the cloak of darkness,
Hopeless but trying to escape the spite
Of a society run on honour and love

To you everything was game
To you everything is game
With power you assume the right to plunder
With might your imperial right to grab
Obnoxious culture grab!
Still you seek a continent grab!

Draped
In awful sheets
Hidden below bloodied boards
Swung across stormy waves
The raucous joy of receiving stolen blood
Shocked me for over hundreds of years until
I heard the shout *Bring Home our Life!*
I take my freedom!
Now!

Freedom!
Let me escape those dreadful eyes
Those stares and whisperings pierce my soul
The sheer wildness and aloofness of false connoisseurs
Scheming wretched plans to disembowel my essence
My worth isn't on being on your pedestal
I must go home!
Ancestors did not cast me to be a spectacle
By me we spoke
By me we speak to generations long born and gone
And generations yet unborn
The flashing of the *eben*
The slashing of the *ada*
All speak volumes as we celebrate life and caution against evil
I'm going home!
Oh, that I may be touched by blessed clay
Oh, that my children may look at me and hear
The rhythms of the past
And warn against the madness of plunder.

Awake
Breaking from awful bonds
We rise from beneath bloodied boards
Swung across stormy waves
The raucous joy of receiving stolen blood
Your greedy bloodied fangs shocked me for over hundreds of years until
Now
Collectively we shout *Bring Home our Life!*
We take my freedom!
Reparations now!
Now!

After Oil We Flourish

(The Niger Delta isn't a ticking ecological time bomb)

The Niger Delta isn't a ticking ecological time bomb
The bomb has already exploded
Shrapnel fly everywhere
In the land, in the water and in the air
The living have long been sacrificed

Today we dream
We dream of a delta teeming with fish and diverse sea foods
We dream of a delta sparking clean creeks, streams, rivers, and the sea
The creeks were mirrors that echoed our joy
We dream of mangroves whose stately roots held our ground and
brought us fish
We dream of days when we pulled on the oars to the tune of
beautiful songs
We dream of songs of health and life today replaced by songs
of survival and death

Sixty years ago, when oil was found in commercial quantities
There was joy and plenty of dreams
Sold on tales of shinny homes, hospitals, schools
Regaled with stories of the banishment of hunger and sundry value
additions to our bustling harvests
We danced, celebrated, quaffed palm wine, and sacrificed some goats
With no clue we were in line to be sacrificed

The footprint of oil had already been stamped on these shores
But that was over palm oil
When palms slapped jaws and foreign merchants
And mercenaries burnt down Akassa way back in 1895
To exploit the market with no sense of responsibility
Or accountability

Fast forward to 1995
And the gallows of the Port Harcourt prison
Choked Ken Saro-Wiwa, a man of peace, and 8 top Ogoni leaders
And thousands more
At the pleasure of the jackboots and drillers
Empowered by war laws that ultimately threw up war lords

The prophet decried the ecological assault on his community
He even declared that the polluters will one day be in the dock
And the docks have since come calling
You cannot hide oil spills by turning the soil
Or by burning our forests and creeks

Once upon a time
Port Harcourt was known as the Garden City
It was a place of gardens, of beauty, the good life, and dance
Today it is the soot city
Covered by a blanket of carbon
From gas flares, decrepit refineries, and heinous bush refineries
COVID-19 social distancing forbids handshakes
But the soot had already banished
Who could dare shake hands coated by soot?
Throats choked, lungs filled
We can barely whisper a salutation
The soot knows no geographic limits
While the mafia stoke their deadly fires
And the security forces smash and lit their own fires
The swamps and creeks and streams

The soot suits no one
Kids choke
Adults suffocate
Babies are born ahead of time
Because some folks think of cash and not the people or the land
Because some folks care nothing of the fact that we all share the
same toxic air

Sad, is it not, that the Niger Delta
Once one of the cleanest places on earth
Has become one of the most polluted places on earth?
Gas flares
Oil spills
Well blowouts
Rotten pipelines
Irresponsible polluters and their collaborators
Point oily fingers at the victims
While oil is syphoned in ocean going vessels
They blame villagers who skim crude from the surface of their creeks
as medicine for convulsions

Welcome to the Niger Delta
Where thanks to fossil fuels exploitation and crass neglect
Funerals now present festivals
As children become elders
Because pollution has stolen their parents

But dreams don't die when we dream awake
Looking at the horizon we see hope
We see a once beaten people liberated
Standing for self determination
Breaking the claws of oppression
We see the linking of hands and the stomping of feet to the rhythms
of hope
As our mothers replant the mangroves
And the polluters decommission their death traps
And the periwinkles and oysters return
And the world wakes to the truth that the age of fossil fuels must
now be fossilized

The Niger Delta isn't a ticking ecological time bomb
The bomb already exploded, but we are here
The harms inflicted repaired by a people determined to live
On the land, in the water and on the air

We are the living
Long committed to telling a story of resilience and self
Determination
Morning comes
After oil

A Dirge for Fossil Capitalism

Having lived millions of years
In the bowel of the Earth
With occasional forays to the surface
You lent yourself to be used as mortar
And sometimes tar
Sometimes you trapped folks in pits as in Sodom and Gomorrah
But finally, some clever folks penetrated your store houses
Of coal, oil, and gas
Donated by matter dead many times over
Today you groan, gripped in death throes
And as you trigger this dirge
We peep at the atrocious paths
Clawed by humans to make you spurt
Capital that tore humanoids apart

Your lines cut through forests, sand dunes and creeks
Claws sunk kilometres deep into oceans
Exploding sound bombs to reverberate off the bellies and backs
of whales
Sounding boards with muffled wails
And friendly seismic data yielding deadly bombs
Nothing, nothing was sacred to you except cash
You cared less when the feet of babes ceased to patter
And your feet turned the Earth into a canvass of craters
Disembowell, the Earth yielded your secrets
And petrodollars and military shields emboldened your
bloody insolence

Today we recall when humans ran amok
Disposed of steam
Soon lost steam
And hoisted internal combustion dragons
Dispensed with solidarity
Took on individuality

Took on insularity
Lost all sense of pluriverses and got stuck in monoculture
    and universities
You were hailed as the harbinger of progress
You knew you were the purveyor of death and destruction
Mine pits, oil wells, flow stations, and gas flares
Infernal stuff than the world ever saw
Yet you thrived undeterred and well defended by deniers
Deflecting truth and roasting the Earth

Today who would remember that you were born around 1900?
A mere infant in the measure of time
You present yourself as the inevitable lord of the planet
Definer of life
Powered by exploitation, subjugation, dispossession, slavery,
    colonialism
Imperialism and putrid capitalism
But here you lie on your deathbed
Beloved of speculators, tycoons, and riders on the horses of greed
You lie, surrounded by liars unable to believe that you could go
The way of all civilizations that negate the wellbeing of Mother Earth
But here you lie, limp, entangled by your bloated
    transnational entrails

Today your bedchambers burst in flames powered by
    wandering methane
Your entrails blackened by soot, like the nostrils of infants
    you choked
The canaries fall silent, benumbed by your evil
Your gas furnaces still echo the hellish dreams of Dante
And we marvel on how you attained this infamous gory depth in the
    slice of time you held humans captive
The diseases you spurned in sacrifice zones remain stuff of legend
The lives you truncated recall your evil reign in a billion tombstones
Your fossil priesthood reinforced your cultic grip
Climate denial the unyielding creed

Net Zero heroes – all traders in hot air
Indirect capturers, rock cavern privatised prisons in the belly
of the Earth
Today each belch marches your toxic farts
Tectonic convulsions expose
Carbon slavers, sequesters and COALonisers that
Kept humans blind as they trudged to the precipice
Risking a plunge into oblivion
Placing a bet on the lie that your false coded farts had bases in Nature

Today as you take your last breath
We blow the horn and announce the passing of the lord of capital
As humans wake up from slumber and stand together,
labour together
Sing together and dance together
As your life support is pulled off by solidarity
Of the children of Mother Earth
Ready to blow your dust into the storm
We behold the rainbow heralding a calm
As we prepare to ensure that your dust never regroups
And regain our mind and recall when we were intertwined
In the community of beings

Return to Being

The battle rages
Who must gobble up the carbon budget,
Wrap Mother Earth in endless bales of smog?
Whose task is to pile the climate debt
And whose lot to be the carbon slave?
Colonize the biosphere
Obliterate the ethnosphere
Hopes mapped in colonial geographies of death
Scarified for sport, boobytrapped and floating on blood

Burst the funeral drums,
Tighten the tourniquets on hard hearts ensconced in hard hats
Drain the pipelines of caked memories and know
Fancy names for deadly scourges never made them friendly
Not Ebola. Not novelty in novel coronavirus
What children have I spawned, Mother Earth groans
The commons enclosed, entrapped for delicate, bloodied
  trophy hunters
Civilized kids hooked on zoos incarcerate relatives for a touch
  of the wild
All game snatching bread from astonished mouths of orphans
Now all masked, suited and 7 billion jabs against zoonotic embraces

Hear the footsteps from the receding market squares
Are you too far gone to hear?
Hear the rumblings of resistance to naked market forces
That roasted habitats and habitations
Lands, seas and skies grabbed yet dreams cannot be corralled 'cause
Daughters of the soil are ever alert, awake, hoisting the sky
And its watery dusts
Knowledge demonised by demons of market environmentalism
  and brazen extractivism
As the hunter's bag becomes a weapon of mass destruction

Bulging pockets hack horns and tusks and an array of idiotic
aphrodisiacs for limp brains
Slithering across the Savannah, stomping on our ancestral hearths
Shall we look, exiled, silent, sullen, sunk and annihilated as our trees
metamorphose into carbon sinks?

The dream is gone, the cock has crowed,
The betrayer seeks a branch to ape a pendulum swing
And one or two shed a tear for the press
As the hawk glides softly on the winds of the dirge seeking a hapless
prey
Funeral drums burst by pulsating biceps of pain
Flutes whisper a dirge long forgotten suddenly emerging from the
depths of years of erased histories
As daughters and sons of the soil pick up pieces of sacred hills, rivers,
forests
Mother Earth awakes, embraces her visible and invisible children
And finally humans return to being

Climate Debt Long Overdue

Climate Debt, an overdue debt
You want to know
If and when the Climate Debt will ever be paid
When will the debtors agree there is a bill?
Could be soon... Could also be later

Don't you see?
Can't you yet perceive it?

Like the Natural Mystic
Probably a **Climate Lockdown**?
A stormy knockdown to wake us up?
Why are we so stuck up
Why do we imagine we are so strong

Don't you see?
Can't you yet perceive it?

By adorning a sunny crown
A tiny virus with Martian suction landing pads
Craves unwary nostrils, mouths and eyes
Made superpowers powerless
Powerless, like in powerless

Don't you see?
Can't you yet perceive it?

Climate lockdown
Could be sooner
No, not later
With or without a crooner
Do not here mention corona

Don't you see?
Can you yet still not perceive it?

Poetry in the time of pandemic

Slash petrol price to zero...
Who senses the fumes of fleeting cash?
Who stocks up gasoline in a season of hunger?
Knock-down price at lock-down time makes
No difference
When
We are going nowhere.

(poetry in the time of pandemic. Add your verses...)

We must breathe again

Social distances widen
As physical distances shrink
As the knees of the murderous cops
Dug into the neck and body of George Floyd
And a law-destroying accomplice held him down with his eyes
Ears blocked against our pleas

I can't breathe!

As the fires flash
As the bullets fly
As murderous dogs
And never-heard-off-weapons of destruction are unleashed
From the white-washed-house of weapons of hate
They must hear our shouts

I can't breathe!

Flights of fancy, flags of disgust dock the orbits above our heads
As citizens black and white, yellow and red
With others far and near
Kneel in solidarity
Against racism
Against slavery
Against colonialism
Against imperialism
Declaring

I can't breathe!

"Until the philosophy
Which hold one race superior and another
Inferior
Is finally

And permanently
Discredited
And abandoned
Everywhere is war
Me say"

I can't breathe!

Fists in the air
We kneel in solidarity
A collective push for international solidarity
And declare: never again
Will the virus of hate and racism
Take away the breath of our people

We must breathe again

2 June 2020

Net Zero Comes to Zero

Extreme climate stands at the door
Record temperatures
Boiling oceans, cyclones and deaths
Shrinking ponds, parched lands
And a smiling line-up of power drunk deniers

Climate inaction a hellish creed
Extreme avoidance of action intensified
Voluntary modes activated for climate inactions
Nothing but sophisticated mathematical acrobatics
Net zero pathways

Youths to whom tomorrow belongs resist
Communities' lands stolen by floods, swelling seas and raging deserts

Question is what does the voluntarism add to
The world has no history of cooperation
History is replete with conflicts, conquistadors,
thieves and murderers

Yet, cooperation is in the memory of humans
The only sure tool for survival is watching each other's back
It means each person carrying her fair share
And not offset loads by wishful thinking

Your ambition aims at 1.5 or well below 2 degrees
And well below hits below the belt of the victims long discounted
But greed and profiteering vacuous pledges point at 3 degrees
Or more
You are bent on
Incinerating the planet

While pretending that persons displaced by climate impacts are
not refugees
You pen beautiful theses on how the Geneva Convention
Set definitions of a refugee in untouchable concrete
Such is the stuff of tyranny and selfishness

Today I am displaced
Today I am scorched,
Today I am cooked by the sun

Tomorrow
You will be
And the papers of your mathematics
The papers of your definitions, conventions and outrageous selfies
with
Your celebrated deals and mis-agreements and net zero
Comes to zero
As you miss the net
And get hit by balls
Of fire

Loan me a slice of lemon

I'm certain you did not hear me
When I squeezed a slice of wisdom
Like you squeeze a slice of lemon
Through parched lips
Into your hungry ears

Come
Back at night
If you want cheap stuff
Snatch your deals from
Between the lips of noisy house flies

My skill of hearing a thousand conversations
At the same time
Capacity to listen individually to a thousand tales
At the same time
I am your expert haggler
In the marketplace of drifting hopes

Learn wisdom
Know how teeth and tongue
Coexist in symbiotic familiarity
A thousand chumps
A drip drip drip
A cracking sound
A marvelous taste

Come
Back at night
If you want cheap stuff
Come and wave off the departing footsteps
Of traders laden down with deaf buyers

Loan me a slice of lemon
Decongest my clogged ears
And eyes
Quench my thirst and
Wake my memories

Wicked Genes

Peddler of wicked genes, will you slide on gene drives?
Knocking out, annihilating traits and yellowing all fruit flies?
Have you considered the many techie graveyards littered with DDT, Agent Orange and all?
Malaria will not be an excuse for you to unleash on our already broken backs

You create a poison and sell the antidote
You create a virus and market anti-virus

Don't crush my cultural webs, ecosystems and bio diversities
Just because you can spit in Mother Earth's face
Trample on Genesis
And flaunt genetically modified technocrats

HIV-AIDS, Ebola, Zika...
Scratch your pouch and unleash some more

We see through your shady genetic scissors, errors and terrors
Your hypothetical benefits drowned in oceans of unquestionable risks
Time it is to break your addiction to crooked technofixes cause our DNA is not for sale,
Nor are we guinea pigs for your gene driven exterminator technologies

The lands we fight to own

Clinging on the face of the wind
I slithered on the waves of the rock
Eardrums assaulted by the sweet sounds of yesteryears
Amazed by the absent soils I peer
At rooftops knowing that
In a short while the concrete piled under the roof
Would have been swept
Into the Pacific and the
Atlantic
Humbling isn't it
Can you see
That the lands we fight to own
Is owned by the sea

Tenants of Furious Times

We could barely hear the whisper
Amidst the thunderous whimper
Emitted before the choristers croaked twice
And the humble fellow's shout thrice scrapped the floor
We could barely see the head
Of our humbled humble man
As hired minstrels mingled with dangerous dancers
And the captive crowd managed a humble clap
That roused a dozing rooster
Who muttered a cracked crow
And followed with another for good measure.
How do you snap explosive whispers
Sound years since the big bang
Or perhaps a smaller bang
In clogged ears of mere
Tenants of furious times

Dreadful Liars On Heartless Shores

Corporatized consciences
Think little of spreading fires
Dreadful liars
Selling adaptation suits for funeral pyres
3 degrees
5 degrees
7 degrees
Flamethrowers watch the Planet burn
As fireworks herald the New Year so a
Flaming Planet announces the arrival of new species
In islands of belly-churning opulence
Fed by blood from multiple zones of sacrifice

Corporatized consciences
Think little of spreading fires
Dreadful liars
Throwing burst life boughs to drowned lands
3 degrees
5 degrees
7 degrees
Lives matter nought
Once fat cats are sated
Other lives don't matter
Give us today fade out
Survival for future games
In lost memories of tomorrow

Corporatized consciences
Elastic tongues propose offset fires
Peddlers of dreadful lies
That though we be charred we aren't burned
3 degrees
5 degrees
7 degrees

Fat cats hooked on power
Can't stand the heat? Try the cold
Can't stand the fragrance of the displaced?
Erect Apartheid Walls to enclose privilege
Populate the media, float belly-up
On barricaded heartless shores

Our Time

We Planted a Flag

We planted a flag
Not on the moon
We are on the lips of
The village long swallowed by the sea
We planted a flag
Waving to memories of
Water wells long swallowed by the sea
We planted a flag
A totem to determi-
Nation
To hold back the rising tide
Keep fossils in the ground
Halt CO2lonisation of our seas
And skies and lands
We planted a flag
Not on the moon
We are sons & daughters of
The soil, the air, the sea
We are here
Present or
Absent
We are here

Welcome to the Age of Paradox

Welcome to the age of paradox
Baskets over our mouths
Masks on forlorn faces we march incognito
Hopes bloom, blossom but long awaited fruits wither
In storms and ambush at corners behind rusty barometers and
wind vanes
Shouts for help blocked by impregnable social distancing
Walled national borders stand silly policed by benumbed sentinels
While viruses float over visa-less air
Naval armadas boast ballistic missiles yet sailors are locked in
by unseen enemies
A cough, a shiver raises dusts and ... a hail of demonic pans
in a pan...demic
This virus floats in the air, slithers on shinny steel and grainy boards
Yet as our fingers hover and minds flutter
No one says for how long the devious virus lives on keyboards
Welcome to the age of paradox

Welcome to the age of paradox
Where were we when the birds chirped the message and
Lizards nodded in prodigious assent
Bellies bulging in agreement and receding in doubt?
Yet in a maddening non-choleric season
We accumulate shit papers rolled in watery dreams
Herd mentality entrenched by fear of the known
Politicians turn conductors of tragic orchestras belting out
an unending dirge
Bust social safety nets torn by goodwill
Trillions were thrown on rusty guns, grenades and jammed hardware
Billions doled to imaginary poorest of the poor that none could sight
no matter where you look
Pandemic of corruption erupts in millions of innovative streaks
Welcome to the age of paradox

Welcome to the age of paradox
Since accumulation remains the creed even in a season of death
Today we wonder if home is where the heart is
Why the restless feet sliding from locked door to locked door
Seeking a break to jump into the brutish
Embrace of brutes in jackboots who had forgotten their heart at loveless homes
Licensed to roam the streets and threaten daughters, mothers and wives with poisoned arrows beneath their belts
In the gloom and the doom
The rich and power brokers once proud of being peripatetic now deny their vagabond history
But all end at the same dilapidated rat infested gates
Of illness clinics they refused to fund
Welcome to the age of paradox

Welcome to the age of paradox
No search warrants, no docks, no pleadings to their lordships
No judgements, yet the world is sentenced
Locked down, locked in, locked up
Terror as running noses paralyse motion
And a mere sneeze shames star olympians
Locked down, locked in, locked up, locked out
We attend parties of the mind and throw banters in the air
Spiders spin intricate webs beneath swivel chairs
And workers speak keyboard to keyboard
Minds sanitised, shut eyes opened with
Hands trapped under running water from long dried faucets
Welcome to the age of paradox

Welcome to the age of paradox
Emptied of corona-virus bats now sleep by night
Men loaded down wheeze and doze in the crack between day and the night
But if bats birthed the pain, why are men still bent on stealing their homes?

Habitats vanish, species go extinct, yet 10 humans are trapped in
3×3m boxes!
What if Coronavirus is your Frankenstein or the genie that escaped
the cork?
Hidden amazements torment our hearts
As these our relatives evicted from their homes
Seek habitations and knocked on our doors
Cashless society starves while cash gets stoked in billionaires'
bottomless pockets
Gate keepers shout the world's population must be cut by 15 per cent
Way to knock off the stats that their wealth equals that of the
rest of the world
Why don't the rich line their golden necks on the slaughter slab
Or be the first to be vaccinated against the virus of greed?
Welcome to the age of paradox

Encrypted

Since I intercepted a cryptic call between trees
I have not stopped tapping my ears on every root
That strays above ground

Since I interpreted encrypted tweets between two sparrows
I went on to regale my peeps with tales from hawks, sunbirds
    and parrots
Until signals from owls strayed into my ears

Owls don't howl as you know
Their sad eyes hide deep secrets related in steady hoots
That send shivers down the spine of non initiates

Since I figured the screech of grasshoppers in the field
I had a field day chasing after butterflies perched on their
    colourful wings
Till I found the most loaded sound is in the silence between flaps

Nigeria

If there is egwu eke
There must be a drummer
Or the flutist
Where there is a dance there must be a song
Who is the musician to whose beat
The python is dancing?

The crocodile please
My gaping jaws and fearsome teeth
Never mean I smile
No matter how hard my stinking efforts with
Dirt-crusted teeth
Who says the crocodile smiles or this a search for flesh to rip?

Whose beat demands a dance?
Whose dance demands a smile?

To question the wisdom of beasts of the forests and of the creeks
The hunted must pause to unravel
When infantries turned into reptiles

No cocky croc grimace
No wiggly cobra twists
Demilitarize
Now!

Africa

Drumbeats drowned
by merchant gunboats
Exploited
Partitioned with a ruler
Rigged with sit tight rulers
Fragmented
Sucked
Sapped
Dried
Burnt
Exposed to subhuman bondage
Time to pushback
Merge the sub nations
One Africa

No cocky croc grimace
No wiggly cobra twists
Demilitarize
Now!

I Have Been in Motion

I have been in motion
Loaded with heavy
baggage of emotion
Bent and bruised
I hesitate to Offload
Any of this On you.
Tight lipped I stammer
Stutter even And add lip
Hole poked
Alibis.

I stay In motion
On my lane
Outpaced by
Talkative Marathoners
Thirsty yet Running
Hamstrung Yet steely
And Steady.
I wander wondering
When I can breast
This tape To end
This race
To your Heart.
Would it
Be quicker
If
I should
Race
On your
Lane?
And if
I were
The
Referee?

Riding the Waves of Time

Riding the waves of time
Surfing the tides of seasons
Pondering the invisible calendars
We cannot... must not adjust
Seasons locked in history
Today!
We rise with deep gratitude
To Him
And to you
And all our relatives
Moving on two, on four or a dozen
Feet

Becoming Clearer

As I get older
It becomes clearer

The things I don't know
Outnumber the things I know

As I get older
It becomes clearer

The things I can't fathom
Outweigh the things I have known

As I get older
It becomes clearer

The lights I haven't seen
Outshine the ones I have seen

As I get older
It becomes clearer

The sounds I haven't heard
Outplay the ones I have heard

As I get older
It becomes clearer

The places I haven't held
Outlast the things I can hold

As I get older
It becomes clearer

The tales yet untold
Outclass those that can be told
As I get older
It becomes clearer that we can go anywhere and not get lost
In the labyrinth of our mind

Time Comes

Time comes
When the pollen
Grains and the leaves and
Fruits adorn your head and
Feet and you are
Grounded beneath contesting
Bush mangoes
Watched by
Chirping birds and myriad creepy crawlers
You know,
Time you must know
We are one with
Mother Earth

When Your Clock Tick Tocks

Gaze at the fleeting years
Slide on nostalgia,
and stubborn memories
in the rear views of life
Mirrors
with many faces and
dreams may be rife
But focus on the perspective
etched by the vista
of converging parallels.
Know that though hopes,
visions,
dreams and
paths ahead
wear enticing apparels
We must know
which and which are
meant for us
Skipping
the needless fights
that raise hear the clock tick tock
be quick
to do things
but know
when to rest.
And
often use
your tongue
to count your teeth
if
by chance
some are left.

I read
a thousand
goodwill messages
all through
yesterday.
Some overwhelming
some astonishing
and
some I'd rather not say.
Then
as I walked through
my lockdown garden
and browsed the verdant bed
The fact
that
you all care
brought home
the fact
that
I am very blessed.

Each passing year

Each passing year
Makes us pause to hear
Are the days longer
or must we deeply ponder
Are the days getting shorter
Or is it that the struggles are getting hotter?
Has the 1% increased
Or has somehow the 99% been squeezed?
I rolled these on my mind all of yesterday
I got even more convinced we must not sway
And when your birthday wishes kept rolling in
And some are yet to arrive, but no, they wont be dropped in the waste bin
we need all the energy to press on and not give up
And your solidarity, love and care ensures we must not stop

What can I say now but THANK YOU

Hasta la victoria siempre!

2/06/2015

Rainbows Through the Tears

It is exactly at a time
when mass graves
Line the streets
as grim markers
of a stubborn
invisible foe
That we understand
the need to appreciate
little graces.

It is precisely at a time

when we hug

and even cry in pity
That we must arise

and see sparkling rainbows

through the tears
And in the midst of

all the pandemonium

behold

unspeakable beauty

It is about the time

when we quicken our pace
To escape the fangs

of racism and

xenophobic tendencies
That's the time to

join our hands

and strengths

and declare

we are one human

race.

Okay to say "all lives matter"
but what's wrong
with being a witness
To the truth that
Black Lives Matter
and that the knee
on that neck
for 9 minutes
less some seconds
Could not be hidden
by any sort of
political correctness
It is exactly at a time

when mass graves
Line the streets

as grim markers

of an invisible

but stubborn foe
That we understand
the need to appreciate

our little times

and

spaces

We are Seeds

Fence a piece of the earth.
Title deeds entitle delusions.
We own nothing.
Everything owns us.
We are seeds
Planted.
We sprout, blossom, bud.
We feed birds, beasts, fish.
Birds, beasts, fish feed us.
We eat them.
They eat us.
We are everything.
Everything is us.
We wake from delusions

Living Earth

Cranks see nature
As distinct from culture
Just as they see human
As different from other-than-human
These same fellows or call them
Felons
Reject human agency
In any historical way responsible
For the ecological changes running riot
Insisting the horrors are caused by impersonal
And invisible market forces
Curable not on surgical beds
But on heated carbon stock exchanges.
Felons see nature
Dead, awaiting scavengers
Vultures, hyenas, ravens
Purifiers of bloated filth
From the imperial hearths
But Mother Earth is a living entity
Teeming with billions of living beings
Weaving trillions of complex tails
Warning through the voices of trees, birds, fishes and more

We can plant a seed

Way back yesterday
In the glow of nighttime fires
We sat around steamy bowls
Carving up mounds of foo foo
Then dipping our hands in hot soups
Mouths long open await the feast
With every bite our tongues knew the source
Jolly jolly bellies, happy happy hearts
We danced our way through the night
These days we line up at the shops
Awaiting junk foods and maybe small chops
Bright coloured walls and blinding lights
We take selfies as we down deadly sodas
With loud music, we munch and munch but hear no crunch from our plastic foods

We can plant a seed
And not eat poison

These days we go to the farm
It could also be the harvest is next to our homes
Straight bananas
Squared up squash
Cassava tubers that don't ferment
Genetic engineers target our staple crops
Especially ones grown by women
With mythic tales they sell lies
Crops kill pests and innocent species
Like their ancestors sold beads, mirrors and whiskies
And we are to be excited eating pesticides
And wash down with water packed in plastics and served like drugs

We can plant a seed
And not eat poison

We live in the city
Streets blocked with cars
Every piece of land thoroughly cementified
The Earth is denied rain from the sky
You want some water, toxic drains send a deluge
We want some corn?
Go to the shop
You want vegetables?
Go to the shop
"This food is safe"
That's what they say
Made by giant conglomerates
On the back of imperial neocolonial agencies
But they cannot even say what they sell
All they yell
Is "shut up and eat
"An hungry man has no choice"
Genetically engineered
Isolated from weeds with glyphosate

We can plant a seed
And not eat poison

All around us seeds are sprouting
Along the rivers and streams through our cities
Every city block long abandoned
Day and night we sow the seeds
Many don't ask where magical fresh foods emerge
We labour all day to bring yet nothing to eat
Officials feed fat on our labours
Then loosen their belts
Call the bulldozers
Pull down our dreams
Level our fields
Destroy our homes
"This urban space isn't for rats

Go back to the village unwanted migrants
Our foods are imported, packaged, some Even come as aid"
We can plant a seed
And not eat poison
The food we eat must not eat us
Mother Earth warns: we are all her children
The plants, the birds, the beasts, the worms, the bees, the butterflies
In the soil and above the soil
On the seas and beneath the seas
Trillions of our relatives call to us
"Globalize the struggle
Globalize hope!"
Globalize the people
Not transnational corporations
Resilience
Solidarity
Hope
Power
Life
are all in the seed
And if we care we can touch the soil
We can plant a seed
We can water a plant
We can nurture life
We can raise a goat
We can connect to the soil
And allow Mother Earth to feed us all

We can plant a seed
And not eat poison

In the Shadows of the Future

(For Jay Naidoo & Stephen Pittam)

In a hide-away in Rustlers Valley
Lodged where the EarthRises to meet the mountains
Drawn by the call of caves and waterfalls
Enraptured by the pull of ancestral footsteps
Sucked into the silence of wisdom
Etched in the solidity of memories long grafted in our blood
We knew we were here thousands of years before
Humbled
We stooped
We rose
And beheld far flung horizons
Future Africa etched in a rocky vista
Global and Greengranting
Hope and solidarity
Poli poli

Things start from the bottom
Yet many prefer the summit
With eyes set at the pockets
Ladders kicked to secure lonely spots
Alone, encrusted in gold and diamond debris while
Folks at the bottom drown in acid mine drainage and still
Buffoons in power relish their tango in gilded caskets

In a hide-away in unnamed valleys
Taunted by numerous sunsets men celebrate
Burials in twisted metallic mind-sets
Dozing blinded by blinkers of exaggerated self-glory
Blind to
Soft trees
With roots tucked in stubborn soils
Split rocks
Yes, we are soft saplings

On the edges of the future
Ears pressed to the rocks we hear
Ancient rhapsodies we hear
Unspoken questions wafting in the air
Which is firmer as you ponder this mountain
Grass or rock?

Beholding solid shadows
We hear the oft whispered queries as
Hearts pump as we ponder the mountains of life
Are you ascending?
Are you descending?
What is the spiral locked in your DNA?
Standing in silence we
Untwist our minds as we
Stand at liberty at the feet of Mother Earth as we
Eliminate blinkers of exaggerated self-glory we
Know that saplings
With roots hooked in stubborn soils
Will split the most stubborn rocks
Poli poli

As we ponder the shadows and the cracks
This poem will be finished...
In the valley or
on the mount

What is in that Barrel?

What is in that Barrel?
What are you carrying in your barrel?
Is it water or crude oil?
We have slapped you, broken your teeth, still
How do you find voices to quarrel?
With the troops placing their boots on your necks?

We breasted your invisible naked wires
Drawing net-breaking loads of filth
Your regular wares spewed into our creeks
We never turned the other cheek
In our search for a different future

We breasted your barbed wires
Wondering what Saro-Wiwa thought
As the maniac's noose draped his saintly neck
Where now is the dignity fought for?
Where, the clean waters and lands died for?

The race for life umpired
By environmental racists and vampires
Walking blind, eyes plugged by profits
Sucking in the labours of modern slaves
While feeding bottomless throats offshore

We breasted your rotten pipes and dragon flames
Wondering what the living think
As their feet sink
In your putrid mess
And dance off with puny rents from your toxic wares

We confront the terrors of your market forces
Never awed by your corporate antisocial irresponsibility
We must tear down your prisons of free trade zones

Breaking your manacles, we arise, free,
Unstoppable by your evil greed

What are we carrying in our barrel?
Is it water or crude oil
How do we find voices to question
With jackboots on our necks?
You forget we have two cheeks and the third blow
must come from our fists

No More Sins to Confess

Contrite, I shuffle to the confessional
And kneel silent at the box
'Cause all evils are accepted as good
I search and scrape my brain
Yet nothing pops up to count as sin
Now I wonder why I wandered here

White and black: hues of same coin
Normal to kill
Normal to waste
Normal to steal
Normal to pollute
Normal to erode
Normal to grab lands, seas and even the air
Dead fish bop and the stench is loved

Contrite, I look around
A lone penitent before the confessor
'Cause all are out on a ride
Where nothing is sacred and
Boundaries are as thin as a pin
Nothing pops up to count as sin
Now I wonder why I wandered here

Displacing the poor
Deforestation without care
Pushing non-productive seeds
Exporting environmental costs
Using, discarding and trashing stubborn plastics
Moving boundary lines
Degrading soils, air and water
Hooded market forces hound
The Unheeding into debt traps

Contrite, I recall the days when men sinned
And saw the edges of hell
'Cause even the big screen turn blank
As sin cannot be captured on tape
Still nothing pops up to count as sin
Now I wonder why I wandered here

Entice and plunge
Folks in debt
Ignite wars, maim, enjoy the sounds of bombs
As innocents groan under the drools of drones
War games and video games merged as blood
Is nothing but blobs on our smart phone screens
Applause attends every heinous deed
Stunned I wonder what could draw a wince
A thousand ways to inflict pains yet unexplored

I snatch foods out of the mouths of the hungry
I sell orphans for the price of a loaf of bread
Father's wire and blow up daughters as advance emissaries to
heaven's gate
Good turned bad
Bad turned good
Turning oneself over to the law does no good
Because I broke no law

Contrite, I shuffled to the confessional
And knelt silent at the box
Before an astonished confessor
Aghast I searched my brain in vain
But nothing popped up to count as sin
I kneel wondering why I wandered there

Pavements of Shame

The distance between check-in and sit-in is huge
A steeple chase and many lines to cross
The economy line: broad, heavy, thick
The fist class line: thin like the 1%
Power games played with multiple referees

Sometimes the embrace of the machine is warmer
Than the hugs of humans
Humans hug and stab
Bar codes interact: gates open, but
Not all the time

The distance between check-in and sit-in is long
Like the claws of the villain in the horror tale
Snaky lanes
Watchful eyes
A hundred folks ahead of me
Some black, some red, some blue, some yellow, some white
A rainbow on the polished floor guided by aluminum rails

The distance between check-in and sit-in is long
Organised disunited nations before my eyes
Carefree strolls
Heavy measured steps
Memories and hopes collide and explode a million dreams
Each luggage a bag of tales

The distance between check-in and sit-in is long
Unyielding steeplechase
Ten, nine, eight, seven, six, soon my turn
But not so fast, two to go
A young man gets to the belt
Takes off his belt and his pants hit his ankle
Empties his pocket and out bounces an apple

The distance between check-in and sit-in is long
A woman and her baby get to the belt
Any liquids? Mirrors?
Why is the baby's body lotion so huge? 120 grams?
Is it medicinal or limited edition found nowhere else?
A gift from grandma? Drop in the bin!

The distance between check-in and sit-in is long
The steeple chase yields the hurdle looms and
I face the *judge*
Stripped naked by sharp eyes with a thousand unspoken accusations
I plead not guilty but must pass the fiery furnace

Pause

Stripped of all metals
Stripped of all papers
Stripped of belts, shoes, wrist watches
Stripped of my smile,
Still you eye my gold capped tooth

9Feet apart
Exactly on your yellow marks
Hands up in the air
Surrendered and still

I wait

Deliberately you wait
Invisible darts assault my body, satisfied
You beckon me off the dragon
Surprised you detect a metallic plate in my lungs
And wonder how I breathe

But wait, your passport is green
Are you from the land of CAPITAL LETTERED EMAILS? Or,
Could that be an offshoot of
Gadhafi's little book?
Tell me what have you hidden from us?

Shepherded into the dark room
You probe my intestines
Your swabbed my belt
My bags, my laptop and lap bottom
And still you need a swab from my tongue?

I watch you strip me of all metals
I watch you strip me of all papers
I watch you strip off my belts, shoes, watch
I watch you fail to strip me of my dignity
And you watch me walk free
On the pavement of your shame

Dawn in Celleno

Dawn in Celleno
The mist reluctantly lifts
One drop at a time
To unveil the hidden beauty locked beyond the hills
The sun peeps behind the heavy clouds
The glistening lawn tell tales of life
Verdant clumps, ruins of glories past emerge
And a distant cockerel announces the
Dawn in Celleno

Lago di Bolsena

On the shores of Lago di Bolsena
The muse comes in the watery vista
Cafes across the street keep a stream of hibiscus tea
As the privatised island with multiple chapels beckon my iris
Splash
A big fish breaks the calm surface mocking
The fisherman listlessly casting his line a metre away
A big fish breaks the calm to salute the sun
                    Wishing to come ashore
As men splash in the gentle waves
                    Thinking they were fish

Drowned in the Air

Poor dolphin thought he'd smartly leap
out of the sea and leave the waves in a heap
Leap it did but got drowned
in the air when it found
A grumpy man in a tiny boat
Who at same time jumped throwing off his coat
His aim the frozen fin
Of the still dolphin
And as he got sucked into space
The snappers pondered who'd take his place
This was one wretched fisher
Whose baits were easy to pilfer
Whose grunts made the fishes snigger
As his baits were smaller than the smallest finger

Our Mind

Ubuntu

Spoons Clatter
But we don't Scatter
When you Show up
At lunch Time
Because It is not
How much You eat
But how many
Are sharing

Ubuntu!

Join in
Enjoy The bond
On trays Laced
With Joy

Darts hurled by Carbon

(Our Voices Will be Heard in Thunder)

Sometimes I wonder if
The bumps in the air are driven
By the carbon stoked up there from the fires of greed
And sometimes I wonder if polluters believe the lie
The fat lie that some tree calcified by their spunk can suck up
their mess
Or carpeting the oceans with their filthy talons can drain
carbon from the air

Sometimes I wonder what
Glues talkers to their mikes year after year in hollow
thoughtless chambers
To bracket common sense in bold capitals
As conned capitals applaud the dearth of ambition and
Big capital and politicos scorn responsibility and link hands
in treacherous tangos
Celebrating with raucous applause each misstep and slide
into ridicule
And blatant denial that the flood already swept away the poor
While they feed on the blood of the damned in their
Conferences of Pretenders

Sometimes I wonder if
They never see how they hung the Planet on life support
Since Kyoto was thrown to the market
Copenhagen dared not hope and
Durban drubbed Cancun, Doha's dud cheque never
Cashable even at walkout fronts of Warsaw
Lima took the cake poking a rude finger in the eyeballs of liberty
Entombing the fat cats in her Little Pentagon as
Caked bloods of the disappeared wailed for justice and for revenge
even, for
Every backward march towards the brink

Sometimes I wonder if
We deny the future we can
Ignore ancient warnings screaming: think of the past to remember
    the future
Yet the roller coaster rolled on
The merry makers clinked glasses
To Paris then we go. Merci beaucoup.
Let's keep dancing
While lives are snuffed by
Darts hurled on Earth by carbon

I sometimes wonder how
We could celebrate our lack of vision
Despite the tom-toms of *blockupy* and except
Alternatiba will blow open the rigor mortised eyelids of zombie
    politicos
Dangling on swinging ropes of TNCs
And the street turns parliaments where our theses are nailed on
    the doors of oppression
And the flood overturns
The tables of the carbon cash changers, whip the speculators
    screaming:
This house was convoked as a place of multilateral negotiations
    Not a den for bilateral and unilateral thieving pretenders
Cooking up Mother Earth with
Decisions and non-decisions sentenced to have effect in the
    4th generation
While clowns in the land of Myopia keep their 4 yearly electoral crowns

Sometimes I know with that canny knowing
Our raised fists and stomping feet will
Drive those carbon farts right up the backs of the gutless polluters
Yes, our voices will be heard in thunder

Clouds

Clouds do not
becloud
My vision
When I'm above
The clouds
A cumulus mat may
Cut of the scurrying folks
Beneath
The clouds
But
Above is an array
Of things seen
To be seen
Or imagined
Clouds don't dampen
My appetite
The tiny platers
And teeny weeny tumblers
May
But the grains
Tell tales to palates
Trained
To ensure
Fleeting moments
Till you get
Beneath the clouds
And gingerly step on
Mother Earth

No vantage points

Bird's eye view
Could be amazing
If the sight is
Good.
Dimmed
Sights are
No vantage points
If the bird
Sees naught
Beyond its
Wings

Mine our Mind

You say
We must mine
To pile up the dime
And you say
We must mine oil to pay
The debt.
Did you say
We must burn gas
To end energy deficit?
I suspect you are complicit
In the deadly ploy
To rape our lands and slay
If we must mine
We must start this time
With mining our minds
To unearth the truly precious finds

Memories

Memories are more than history
Memories tell more than tales of misery
Memories are not scrapbooks of experiences
Memories speak loudly even in silences
Memories can be accusatory
Memories demand we tell our story
Memories insist that today is built on past presences
Memories expose needless attempts to enforce absences
Memories remind us that we can't fight our fights alone
Memories expose the futilities of pretending you are a mere clone
Memories tell what our land was in the past
Memories show that we must reflect and act fast
Memories ensure we stand for what will last
Memories may be tough but the delineate or task
Memories open up injuries some may cover
Memories show that together we have the power
Memories say never forget
Memories warm that if you do you are on the highway of regret
Memories ask what do you remember?
Memories demand that on justice we must ponder
Memories say don't forget pillory
Memory demands we don't repeat hurtful history

Blown on High Street

Walking among the crowd on this city street
Squashed, I slice through the mammoth throng
Swaying from side to side helps none
Weaving through the endless wave
Taking in the sights
Of countless dreams
The concrete towers reaching towering heights
On broken backs of labouring toilers
Block upon block following the builder's fancy
Which birds weave nests on the dreadful balconies?
Hit on every side by wafts of heinous smoke
Issues from leafy bits wrapped in innocent sheets.
On an innocent stroll will I get stoned
Lifted sky high beyond the clouds
A crime to hit high the stones of high street?
At every corner a drifting soul
Teary eyed
wheezing sunken cheeks
Vacant bellies and haunted souls
Soaked by unforgiving drafts
Lifted higher on every step
Minds blown
By burning leaves
On blurbing lips.
Thought the devil was bound to Hell's Kitchen
But freely he roams the most Broad Way.
Quick get me to the narrow street
Don't blow my mind on high street.
Why should I be stoned
On your cold street
When
I'm no party for secondhand smoke?

I Catch Myself

You can't catch me
I am faster than a blink
Twinkling faster than
The largest chunk
Floating in space
I catch my thoughts
Before they congeal
Into words
I catch my words
Before they coalesce
Into a sentence
I catch my sentences
Before they string
Into a verse
I catch the choruses
Before they stab
The stanzas
I catch myself
Before you catch
Me
I catch myself
Before
I fall

Holding my Peace

I do my best
Not to lose my cool
More than once or twice
A lunar cycle
Even when besieged
By voracious lunatics
I do my best
To hold my peace
But I leave a space
For unending rage
When whole communities
Are criminalised
And sacrificed
For the benefit
Criminal
Exploiters.

Dreams Dissolved

The stump stands
Where once
Was a tree
That stump
Was my perch
Whenever I was stumped.
Ringside seat
On the lips of
Goi Creek
Crude spread on its face
Remnants of dwellings
Marked by stubborn charred
Remains of rafters and posts
The tides lick
The earth
Chews the chikoko
Banishes dreams of mudskippers seeking
A return
Or the crocs imagining a
Reincarnation
In Goi Creek
Fumes sting my ices
As oily tears
Evoke fears
For the lads cat wheeling
In the mire
And the fisherman tears
The belly of the tilapia
To reveal crude
Oil
The devils dart
The emblem of pain
Of futile labour
The grim reaper

Insatiate eater
Of our relatives
Our cousins and
Of all that is good.
Today I stand
Aghast
Stumped
My perch is gone
Swallowed by the unyielding tides
Dreams
Dissolved
In the mire
I stand here
On your bed of sludge
Knowing we must
Speak
We must act
Before we
Become we are washed
With our dreams

Traps Sold on Lies

Traps are engineered to fly
Call necked but oft exposed when perforated
Have you ever been trapped by a lie?
Garnished, shinny, decorated
The quicker they fly.

Traps are sold on lies
The more brazen
The more attractive, the more the ties
Those who pretend not to know get taken
Even when laid under open skies.

Entrapped?
By choice
In burrowed robes draped
See the skeletal poise!
Yet some insist it mustn't be scrapped

A thief may be excused
If he stole on the pull of a rumbling stomach
Yet when caught must join the dock of the accused
And like the tyre on the tarmac
The demands of motion can't be refused

Traps are sold on lies
Barefaced fed on toxic beef
Eat my pies
Though you die you'll live
Deadened to pain, anaesthetised by tsetse flies

Traps sometimes suck out thumb-sized brains
Of potentates napping in gilded stately caskets
Insatiate sinkholes choking on endless trains of alien grains
Slurping on treaties laid out in odious rackets
It is time, isn't it, to shove the trap down the drains?

The worst trap isn't the one that caught the deer
Not the one that caught the unwary crocodile
The worst trap is set with a sneer
Nations are sucked in by the roulette dial
The debt trap, that's the death trap my dear

Sinsibere

Lend me a hand
Let me stand
Let me labour
The fruits of my labour

Sinsibere

The sweat of a labouring woman
Births pots laden
With songs, with life
With joy

Sinsibere

Drops of coins
In empty cans may
Shroud calloused hearts
But never quench want

Sinsibere

A stick to aid our rise
The stick to trod the earth
The stick to quench want
The stick on the paths of life

Sinsibere

Stone me not with coins
Let me stand
Let me labour
Let me celebrate
The fruits of my labour

Sinsibere is a Bambara word, meaning the support that someone needs to start something. This poem was inspired by contrasting the active work of the women in the Sinsibere Cooperative at Bougoula to the urban poor extending empty bowls for alms. Written in a car on the streets of Bamako - 01.03.2016

If the Sun Slept

If the sun ever slept
Or maybe took a nap
And the moon stepped out at midday
Would we then see the dark side of the moon?

If the strutting moon came to life
Rather than reflect it blazed like fire
Would the ebbing sun supply a shade
For burning heads, forests and seas?

If the sun loses its shine
And we could gaze at its hollow core
Would the moon roam the sky
Rising from the north and setting at will?

What if the oceans took to the sky
And rain fell without stop
Would the fishes shop for towels or raincoats
Or jump on forgotten beaches with burning towels?

What if the sun dozed a tiny with
And lightyears turn all dark
Taking blinkers off waking eyes
Who would cool a raging moon?

If the sun ever slept
Or the eclipse lasted a zillion years
And the moon takes to teasing the sea of burning sand
Where would be the rides awaited by astonished fisher folks?

Really, if the sun went to sleep
When would be day and when would be night
And who would define the full moon, the half crescent
And that sombre face on the moon?

Poetry titles from Daraja Press

A Mutiny of Morning • Nikesha Breeze

Nikesha Breeze has taken words from Joseph Conrad's *Heart of Darkness* and forced them to leave his colonized mind in a radical, surgical, and unapologetic Black appropriation. The resulting poems are sizzling purifications, violent restorations of integrity, pain, wound, bewilderment, rage, and sometimes luminous generosity.

ISBN-13: 978-1-990263-35-42 • 100 pages • $30 • https://bityl.co/DSZL

Love After Babel • Chandramohan S

Winner of the Nicolás Cristóbal Guillén Batista Outstanding Book Award from the Caribbean Philosophical Association

Love after Babel deals with themes such as caste, the resistance of Dalit people, Dalit literature, islamophobia and other political themes, in almost one hundred poems. The introduction is by Suraj Yengde, award-winning scholar and activist from India.

ISBN-13: 978-1-988832-37-1 • 110 pages • $15.30 • https://bit.ly/3n9yNLr

Love Pandemic • Salimah Valiani

These poems were largely written during the first wave of the COVID-19 pandemic. The last poem in the collection was written at the start of the second wave in Africa. Most were circulated through Whatsapp voice notes, an intimate way of keeping distance while reaching out to touch.

ISBN-13: 978-1-990263-53-8 • 32 pages • $10 • https://bityl.co/DTap

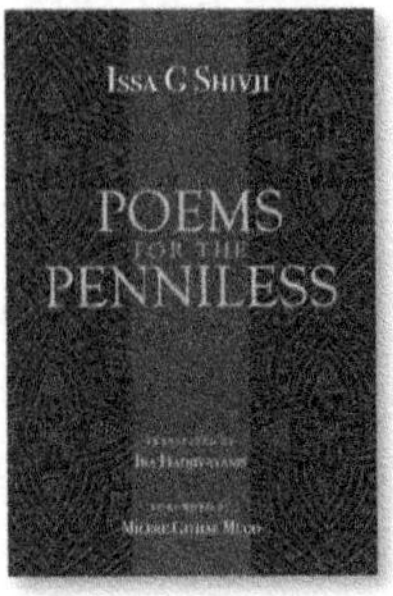

Poems for the Penniless • Issa G Shivji

These poems by Issa Shivji, lawyer, activist and Tanzanian public intellectual, were written at different times in different circumstances. They give vent to personal anguish and political anger. Mostly were originally written in Kiswahili, here wonderfully translated by Ida Hadjivayanis, they are intensely personal and political.

ISBN-13: 978-1-988832-17-3 • 216 pages • $25 • https://bit.ly/3gue9Ve

Daraja Press

Order from **darajapress.com** or **zandgraphics.com**
Prices in U.S. dollars